ROTTERD.

2023 Travel Guide

Unleashing the Vibrant Soul of the City; Tips, Tricks, and Recommendations for Every Traveler

Betty Vanslyke

Copyright © 2023 by Betty Vanslyke

TABLE OF CONTENT

TABLE OF CONTENT

MAP OF ROTTERDAM

INTRODUCTION

CHAPTER ONE

WHY VISIT ROTTERDAM:

QUICK FACTS ABOUT ROTTERDAM:

CHAPTER TWO

GETTING TO ROTTERDAM

AIRPORTS AND TRANSPORTATION OPTIONS

AIRPORTS:

TRANSPORTATION OPTIONS:

CHAPTER THREE

GETTING AROUND

PUBLIC TRANSPORTATION WITHIN ROTTERDAM

CHAPTER FOUR

ACCOMMODATION OPTIONS IN ROTTERDAM

TYPES OF ACCOMMODATIONS AVAILABLE:

RECOMMENDED HOTELS AND GUESTHOUSES:

BUDGET-FRIENDLY OPTIONS:

CHAPTER FIVE

KEY NEIGHBORHOODS AND DISTRICTS

CHAPTER SIX

ICONIC LANDMARKS AND ATTRACTIONS IN ROTTERDAM

CHAPTER SEVEN

MUSEUMS AND CULTURAL INSTITUTIONS

CHAPTER EIGHT

FOOD AND DRINK

DUTCH CUISINE AND LOCAL SPECIALTIES:

MUST-VISIT RESTAURANTS AND CAFES:

FOOD MARKETS AND STREET FOOD:

CHAPTER NINE

SHOPPING AND ENTERTAINMENT

POPULAR SHOPPING STREETS AND AREAS:

UNIQUE BOUTIQUES AND CONCEPT STORES:

NIGHTLIFE AND ENTERTAINMENT OPTIONS:

CHAPTER TEN

EVENTS AND FESTIVALS THAT IGNITE THE CITY

ROTTERDAM UNLIMITED:

INTERNATIONAL FILM FESTIVAL ROTTERDAM (IFFR):

ROTTERDAM ART WEEK:

WORLD PORT DAYS:

CHAPTER ELEVEN

OUTDOOR ACTIVITIES AND PARKS

HET PARK:

KRALINGSE BOS:

ROTTERDAM ZOO AND BLIJDORP GARDENS:

CYCLING AND WALKING ROUTES:

CHAPTER TWELVE

DAY TRIPS FROM ROTTERDAM

DELFT:

THE HAGUE:

KINDERDIJK:

GOUDA:

CHAPTER THIRTEEN

PRACTICAL INFORMATION FOR A SEAMLESS ROTTERDAM EXPERIENCE

WEATHER AND BEST TIME TO VISIT:

CURRENCY AND BANKING:

SAFETY TIPS AND EMERGENCY NUMBERS:

USEFUL PHRASES IN DUTCH:

CONCLUSION

RECAP OF ROTTERDAM'S HIGHLIGHTS

FINAL TIPS AND SUGGESTIONS FOR VISITORS

MAP OF ROTTERDAM

INTRODUCTION

Welcome to Rotterdam, a city that breathes life into steel, where architectural wonders reach for the sky, and creativity knows no bounds. In the pages of this travel guide, we invite you to embark on a journey through the beating heart of Rotterdam, a city that effortlessly blends tradition with innovation, history with modernity, and captivating charm with unyielding resilience.

Imagine a place where the past collides with the future, where historic cobblestone streets intertwine with avant-garde masterpieces of design. Rotterdam is a city that rose from the ashes of destruction, reinventing itself as a vibrant metropolis that pushes the boundaries of imagination. Its daring skyline, punctuated by iconic landmarks, whispers stories of triumph, creativity, and a relentless spirit.

As you turn the pages of this guide, we will unveil Rotterdam's hidden treasures, guiding you through its winding canals, inviting neighborhoods, and pulsating cultural scene. Discover a city where bicycles gracefully weave through bustling streets, where street art adorns every corner, and where a melting pot of cultures adds flavor to every dish.

Uncover the secrets of Rotterdam's world-renowned museums and cultural institutions, immerse yourself in the electric energy of its festivals and events, and indulge in culinary delights that tantalize your taste buds. Let the city's parks and green spaces embrace you in their tranquility, offering a moment of respite amidst the urban hustle.

In this travel guide, we don't just provide you with information, we invite you to become a part of Rotterdam's story. Let the city's vibrant pulse guide your steps as you navigate its neighborhoods, absorb its history, and engage with its passionate locals. Get lost in the beauty of its architecture, its dynamic cultural scene, and the undeniable sense of possibility that hangs in the air.

So, pack your curiosity, open your mind to the extraordinary, and let Rotterdam weave its magic around you. This travel guide is your key to unlocking the hidden gems, the unforgettable experiences, and the soul-stirring moments that await you in the captivating city of Rotterdam. Are you ready to embark on an adventure like no other? Let's dive into the vibrant tapestry of Rotterdam and create memories that will last a lifetime.

CHAPTER ONE

Why Visit Rotterdam:

Welcome to Rotterdam, a city that defies conventions and embraces its unique identity as a vibrant hub of innovation, architectural marvels, and cultural riches. Nestled in the heart of the Netherlands, this captivating destination invites you

to embark on a journey like no other. Picture a place where futuristic skyscrapers coexist with historic windmills, where bustling markets breathe life into the streets, and where a spirit of resilience and creativity permeates every corner. Rotterdam, a city that has emerged from the ashes of World War II, now stands tall as a testament to human determination and the boundless possibilities of urban renewal.

Unveiling the Jewel:

Imagine stepping into a cityscape that blends the old and the new, where sleek glass structures rise from the remains of ancient shipyards. Rotterdam's architectural prowess is second to none, boasting a skyline adorned with avant-garde masterpieces. Behold the majestic Erasmusbrug, an elegant bridge that gracefully spans the River Maas, connecting the city's vibrant heart with the thriving Kop van Zuid district. As sunlight dances on its sleek curves, it is a reminder that Rotterdam is a city perpetually in motion, bridging the gap between past and future.

The Pulse of Culture:

Rotterdam pulses with a cultural beat that resonates in its museums, galleries, and cultural institutions. Enter the hallowed halls of Museum Boijmans Van Beuningen, where masterpieces by Van Gogh, Rembrandt, and other greats beckon you into a world of artistic brilliance. The Kunsthal Rotterdam, a veritable treasure trove of contemporary art, captures the imagination with its ever-changing exhibitions. And for an enchanting encounter with nature, visit the awe-inspiring Rotterdam Zoo, a lush sanctuary where both young and old can marvel at the wonders of the animal kingdom.

A Gastronomic Voyage:

Prepare your taste buds for an unforgettable culinary odyssey through Rotterdam's diverse culinary scene. Sample mouthwatering local delicacies such as freshly caught herring, stroopwafels oozing with caramel, and bitterballen bursting with savory goodness. Wander through the bustling Markthal, a sensory wonderland where flavors from around the world intermingle and aromas waft through the air. Let the bustling food markets and vibrant street food stalls ignite your senses and satisfy your cravings.

The Soul of Rotterdam:

Rotterdam's spirit is not confined to its streets alone; it extends to the hearts of its resilient inhabitants. It is a city where innovation flourishes, where new ideas and startups find fertile ground to grow. The relentless determination of the Rotterdammers, reminiscent of the city's iconic Cube Houses, inspires visitors and locals alike to think outside the box, challenge norms, and create a better future.

Beyond Rotterdam's Borders:

While Rotterdam captivates with its myriad offerings, it also serves as a gateway to neighboring treasures. Venture to Delft, the city of blue and white ceramics, where picturesque canals wind their way through a tapestry of historical charm. Explore The Hague, the political heartbeat of the Netherlands, where grand palaces and world-class museums await your arrival. Or embark on a pilgrimage to Kinderdijk, a UNESCO World Heritage site that showcases the enchanting beauty of windmills standing sentinel over the Dutch landscape.

As you bid farewell to Rotterdam, its indomitable spirit will remain etched in your memory. It is a city that rises above adversity, continuously reinventing itself with unwavering determination. Rotterdam is a testament to human ingenuity and the power of collaboration, where dreams are transformed into reality. So come, immerse yourself in the dynamic tapestry of Rotterdam, and let its allure capture your heart and ignite your imagination.

Quick Facts about Rotterdam:

- Rotterdam is known as the "Gateway to Europe" due to its status as Europe's largest port.

- The city is home to the iconic Rotterdam Central Station, a modern architectural masterpiece.

- Rotterdam is renowned for its annual events, including the vibrant Rotterdam Unlimited Festival and the International Film Festival Rotterdam (IFFR).

- The city embraces sustainability and green initiatives, evident in its many parks, urban gardens, and sustainable architecture.

- Rotterdam's innovative floating pavilions and water management strategies highlight its commitment to combating climate change and rising sea levels.

Intrigued? Get ready to embark on a journey through Rotterdam's dynamic streets, where architectural marvels, cultural delights, and a vibrant atmosphere await at every turn. Discover a city that defies expectations, embraces its past while embracing the future, and invites you to experience the bold spirit of Rotterdam like never before.

CHAPTER TWO

Getting to Rotterdam

Airports and Transportation Options

As you prepare to embark on your journey to Rotterdam, it is essential to familiarize yourself with the various transportation options available to ensure a smooth and convenient arrival. Rotterdam, located in the heart of the Netherlands, boasts excellent connectivity and accessibility, thanks to its well-connected airports and efficient transportation systems. Let's delve into the details of airports and transportation options, ensuring a seamless transition into the vibrant embrace of Rotterdam.

Airports:

Rotterdam The Hague Airport (RTM):

Situated just a short distance from the city center, RTM offers the closest and most convenient option for travelers.

Served by several major airlines, including low-cost carriers, RTM provides both domestic and international flight connections.

With its modern facilities and streamlined processes, this airport ensures a hassle-free arrival and departure experience.

Amsterdam Airport Schiphol (AMS):

While not located in Rotterdam itself, Amsterdam's Schiphol Airport is one of the largest and busiest airports in Europe, offering a wide range of international flight connections.

From Schiphol, travelers can easily reach Rotterdam via various transportation options, making it a viable choice for international visitors.

The airport features excellent facilities, including shops, restaurants, and convenient transportation links to Rotterdam.

Transportation Options:

- **Train:** The train is an efficient and popular mode of transportation between Amsterdam Airport Schiphol and Rotterdam.

  The direct Intercity trains run frequently and provide a comfortable journey, with a travel time of approximately 25 minutes.

  The trains are equipped with amenities such as free Wi-Fi and spacious seating, allowing you to relax and enjoy the picturesque Dutch landscape.

- **Taxi and Private Transfers:** Taxis and private transfers offer a convenient and personalized transportation option from the airports to Rotterdam.

  Taxis are readily available at both Rotterdam The Hague Airport and Amsterdam Airport Schiphol, providing a door-to-door service.

  Private transfer services can be pre-booked, ensuring a smooth and tailored experience, particularly for larger groups or travelers with specific requirements.

- **Public Transportation:** Rotterdam boasts an excellent public transportation system, including buses, trams, and metro lines, making it easy to navigate the city and its surroundings.

  The RET (Rotterdam Electric Tram) operates an extensive network of trams and buses, providing reliable and efficient transportation within the city.

  The Rotterdam Metro, with its comprehensive routes, allows for quick and convenient travel to various parts of the city, including popular attractions and neighborhoods.

- **Rental Cars:** For those seeking flexibility and independence, renting a car is a viable option.

  Multiple car rental agencies are available at both airports, offering a range of vehicles to suit different needs and budgets.

  Rotterdam's well-developed road infrastructure and ample parking options make exploring the city and its surrounding areas by car a convenient choice.

With its accessible airports and diverse transportation options, Rotterdam ensures a seamless and convenient journey for travelers. Whether arriving at Rotterdam The Hague Airport or opting for Amsterdam Airport Schiphol, a range of transportation choices, including trains, taxis, public transportation, and rental cars, are readily available. Embrace the ease of travel and allow the city's efficient transportation systems to whisk you away to the vibrant heart of Rotterdam, where unforgettable adventures await at every turn.

CHAPTER THREE

Getting Around

Public transportation within Rotterdam

Once you arrive in Rotterdam, a world of vibrant neighborhoods, iconic landmarks, and cultural treasures awaits your exploration. To navigate this captivating city effortlessly, Rotterdam offers a comprehensive and efficient public transportation system. With an extensive network of buses, trams, and metros, getting around Rotterdam is not only convenient but also an opportunity to immerse yourself in the city's rhythm and energy. Let's delve into the details of public transportation within Rotterdam, ensuring that every corner of this enchanting destination is within your reach.

- **RET (Rotterdam Electric Tram):** Trams: Rotterdam's iconic trams are a reliable and popular mode of transportation, providing easy access to various parts of the city. The RET operates an extensive tram network, with multiple lines connecting key neighborhoods, attractions, and transportation hubs.

- **Buses:** The RET's bus network complements the tram system, serving areas beyond the reach of trams. Buses run regularly and offer a convenient way to explore Rotterdam's diverse districts, including the outskirts and neighboring towns.

- **Rotterdam Metro:** The Rotterdam Metro is a rapid transit system that efficiently connects different parts of the city. It comprises several lines, denoted by colors, each serving specific areas and attractions.

The metro network extends to both the city center and the outskirts, making it an excellent choice for accessing popular destinations like the Euromast, Ahoy Rotterdam, and Rotterdam Central Station.

The metro operates frequently, especially during peak hours, ensuring minimal waiting times and efficient travel.

- **OV-chipkaart:** To access public transportation within Rotterdam, it is recommended to use the OV-chipkaart, a contactless smart card that serves as a ticket for trams, buses, and metros.

  The OV-chipkaart can be obtained at various locations, including metro stations, and can be topped up with credit for seamless travel throughout the city.

  Simply swipe your OV-chipkaart when entering and exiting trams, buses, or metro stations to deduct the appropriate fare from your card.

- Travel Passes and Tickets: Rotterdam offers various ticket options to suit different travel needs. For shorter stays, consider purchasing disposable tickets or single-use chip cards, available at stations and retail outlets.

Tourists may opt for the Rotterdam Welcome Card, which provides unlimited travel on RET services for a specific duration, along with discounts at museums, attractions, and restaurants.

For longer stays or frequent travel, the personal OV-chipkaart can be a cost-effective solution, allowing you to load credit or purchase season tickets for unlimited travel within specific zones.

Accessibility: Rotterdam's public transportation system is designed to be accessible to all, with facilities for individuals with disabilities or reduced mobility. Many trams, buses, and metro stations are equipped with ramps, elevators, and designated spaces for wheelchair users.

Audio and visual announcements are available on trams and metros, ensuring that information is accessible to everyone.

Integration with Bicycles: Rotterdam is a bicycle-friendly city, and public transportation seamlessly integrates with cycling. Many tram and metro stations provide bicycle parking facilities, allowing you to combine your journey with a bike ride.

You can also take your bicycle on the metro during off-peak hours, enabling you to explore Rotterdam's neighborhoods and parks at your own pace.

Rotterdam's efficient public transportation system empowers you to explore the city's vibrant tapestry with ease. Whether it's hopping on a tram to immerse yourself in the lively streets, traversing the metro to discover hidden gems, or embarking on a bus journey to explore the outskirts, Rotterdam's network of buses, trams, and metros connects you to every corner of this captivating city. Embrace the rhythm of Rotterdam's public transportation, and let it carry you on a journey of discovery, allowing you to uncover the city's rich cultural heritage, architectural wonders, and welcoming neighborhoods.

CHAPTER FOUR

Accommodation Options in Rotterdam

Finding the perfect accommodation is crucial to enhance your experience in Rotterdam. Whether you're seeking luxury, comfort, or budget-friendly options, the city has a diverse range of accommodations to suit every traveler's needs. Join us as we explore the various types of accommodations available, recommend top-notch hotels and guesthouses, and discover budget-friendly options that will make your stay in Rotterdam truly memorable.

Types of Accommodations Available:

- **Hotels:** Rotterdam boasts a wide selection of hotels, ranging from luxurious five-star establishments to boutique hotels and cozy family-run accommodations. Choose a hotel that aligns with your preferences and desired level of comfort.

- **Guesthouses and Bed and Breakfasts**: For a more personalized and intimate experience, consider staying in a guesthouse or bed and breakfast. These establishments often provide a cozy and homely atmosphere, along with warm hospitality from the hosts.

- **Apartments and Serviced Apartments**: Ideal for those seeking a home-away-from-home experience, apartments, and serviced apartments offer the convenience of self-catering facilities and ample space to relax and unwind.

Recommended Hotels and Guesthouses:

- **Mainport Hotel**: This luxurious five-star hotel offers stunning views of the city's skyline and the Maas River. Indulge in its modern design, luxurious amenities, and top-notch service.

- **Hotel New York**: Housed in the former headquarters of the Holland-America Line, this iconic hotel exudes charm and history. Enjoy its waterfront location, elegant rooms, and a sense of nostalgia.

- **King Kong Hostel**: A popular choice for budget-conscious travelers, King Kong Hostel offers stylish dormitory and private rooms, a vibrant atmosphere, and a central location in the heart of the city.

Budget-Friendly Options:

- **Stayokay Rotterdam**: Located in the iconic Cube Houses, Stayokay Rotterdam provides affordable accommodations in a unique architectural setting. Enjoy its communal spaces, comfortable rooms, and social atmosphere.

- **Hotel Bazar**: Offering a vibrant and eclectic atmosphere, Hotel Bazar features uniquely decorated rooms inspired by different world cultures. It provides budget-friendly accommodations with a touch of charm and character.

- **Airbnb**: Rotterdam has a wide range of Airbnb listings, providing budget-friendly options and a chance to stay in local neighborhoods. From private rooms to entire apartments, you can find a comfortable and affordable option to suit your needs.

From luxurious hotels to cozy guesthouses and budget-friendly accommodations, Rotterdam offers a wide range of options to suit every traveler's preferences. Whether you desire a lavish experience at hotels like Mainport Hotel or seek the charm of unique establishments like Hotel New York, there's something for everyone. For budget-conscious travelers, options such as King Kong Hostel, Stayokay Rotterdam, and Hotel Bazar provide affordable comfort and a memorable stay. Consider your needs, budget, and desired experience when choosing your accommodation in Rotterdam, and let the city's hospitality and warmth make your stay truly exceptional.

CHAPTER FIVE

Key Neighborhoods and Districts

Rotterdam, a city teeming with energy and innovation, unveils its vibrant personality through a tapestry of diverse neighborhoods and districts. Each area possesses a distinct character and allure, offering unique experiences that contribute to the city's dynamic charm. Embark on a journey through Rotterdam's key neighborhoods and districts, immersing yourself in their rich history, architectural wonders, artistic hubs, and lively atmospheres.

- **City Center**: The City Center of Rotterdam is the beating heart of the city, where modernity and history intertwine. The iconic Markthal, a colossal covered market hall adorned with vibrant artwork, entices visitors with its culinary delights and bustling ambiance.

Explore the historic Laurenskwartier, home to the impressive Laurenskerk (St. Lawrence Church) and the bustling Lijnbaan, one of the first pedestrian shopping streets in Europe.

Stroll along the scenic waterfront of the Boompjeskade, offering picturesque views of the Maas River and the iconic Erasmusbrug, a graceful bridge that epitomizes Rotterdam's architectural prowess.

- **Delfshaven**: Delfshaven, a charming neighborhood with a rich maritime heritage, transports you to the city's past. It showcases beautifully preserved historic buildings, canals, and cobblestone streets.

  Visit the Delfshaven Harbor, where the Pilgrims' Fathers departed for the New World in 1620, and explore the historic windmill, De Distilleerketel.

  Delfshaven offers cozy cafés, restaurants, and local breweries, making it an ideal spot to savor traditional Dutch cuisine and enjoy the laid-back atmosphere.

- **Kop van Zuid**: Kop van Zuid is Rotterdam's contemporary and architectural masterpiece, located on the southern bank of the Maas River. It boasts a futuristic skyline, dominated by iconic structures such as the Rotterdam Cruise Terminal and the imposing De Rotterdam building.

  The Wilhelminapier, a former harbor area transformed into a cultural hotspot, houses the Luxor Theater and the Nederlands Fotomuseum, captivating visitors with artistic performances and exhibitions.

  Take a leisurely stroll along the Rijnhaven Bridge, known as "The Swan," and soak in the panoramic views of the river and the cityscape.

- **Katendrecht**: Once a rough and tumble neighborhood, Katendrecht has undergone a remarkable transformation and emerged as a trendy and lively district. It exudes a vibrant mix of cultures, showcasing a fusion of cuisines, entertainment venues, and artistic spaces.

Explore the historic Deliplein, a vibrant square dotted with restaurants, bars, and terraces. Indulge in culinary delights ranging from traditional Dutch dishes to international gastronomy.

Visit the Fenix Food Factory, a bustling market hall where local artisans and food producers showcase their products, providing a true taste of Rotterdam.

- **Museumkwartier**: The Museumkwartier is a treasure trove for art enthusiasts, boasting a cluster of world-class museums and cultural institutions. Immerse yourself in artistic brilliance at the Museum Boijmans Van Beuningen, which houses an extensive collection spanning centuries.

Admire the innovative architecture of the Kunsthal Rotterdam, a multidisciplinary art gallery hosting a diverse range of exhibitions.

Explore the Natural History Museum Rotterdam and delve into the wonders of the natural world, from fossils to animal exhibits.

Rotterdam's key neighborhoods and districts encapsulate the city's spirit, inviting you to unravel its multifaceted beauty. From the modernity of the City Center and Kop van Zuid to the historical charm of Delfshaven, each neighborhood weaves its unique story into the vibrant tapestry of Rotterdam. Explore the streets, savor the flavors, immerse yourself in art, and let the dynamic atmosphere of Rotterdam's key neighborhoods captivate your senses, leaving an indelible mark on your journey through this extraordinary city.

CHAPTER SIX

Iconic Landmarks and Attractions in Rotterdam

Rotterdam, a city that embraces innovation and defies conventions, showcases a remarkable blend of modern architecture, cultural treasures, and awe-inspiring landmarks. From futuristic skyscrapers to historical gems, Rotterdam's iconic attractions captivate the imagination and offer a glimpse into the city's dynamic spirit. Join us on a journey through some of Rotterdam's most iconic landmarks and attractions, where architectural prowess, cultural heritage, and artistic brilliance converge.

Erasmusbrug (Erasmus Bridge):

Spanning the majestic Maas River, the Erasmusbrug stands as an iconic symbol of Rotterdam. This graceful cable-stayed bridge connects the northern

and southern parts of the city, offering panoramic views of the skyline and the bustling river traffic.

Admire the bridge's sleek design, resembling a swan in mid-flight, and explore the nearby Wilhelminapier, home to notable buildings such as Hotel New York and De Rotterdam.

Markthal (Market Hall):

The Markthal is a striking architectural marvel that enthralls visitors with its vibrant colors, impressive dimensions, and an exquisite artwork-adorned ceiling. This indoor food market is a haven for food

lovers, featuring a vast array of fresh produce, international delicacies, and culinary delights from around the world.

Marvel at the vibrant murals, indulge in delectable treats and soak in the lively atmosphere of this culinary paradise.

Euromast:

Standing tall as Rotterdam's most iconic observation tower, the Euromast offers breathtaking views of the city and its surroundings. Take a panoramic elevator ride to the top and revel in the stunning vistas, reaching as far as The Hague and even the Belgian coast on clear days.

For the adventurous at heart, dare to take the exhilarating "Euromast's Space Tower" ride, a thrilling descent from the top, or enjoy a luxurious meal at the tower's panoramic restaurant.

Cube Houses:

Rotterdam's Cube Houses (Kubuswoningen) are a

testament to the city's architectural audacity.

Designed by Piet Blom, these tilted, cube-shaped houses create a striking visual spectacle.

Wander through the Kijk-Kubus (Show Cube), a fully furnished cube house transformed into a museum, and gain insight into the unique interior layout of these peculiar residences.

Rotterdam Central Station:

A true architectural gem, Rotterdam Central Station is more than just a transportation hub; it's a

destination in itself. The station's sleek and modern

design, with its soaring roof and expansive atrium, exemplifies Rotterdam's commitment to architectural innovation.

Explore the station's shops, restaurants, and art installations, or marvel at the impressive view from the rooftop terrace.

SS Rotterdam:

Step back in time and explore the SS Rotterdam, a former ocean liner turned floating hotel and museum. This magnificent vessel offers a glimpse into the golden era of transatlantic travel, with preserved cabins, lavish public areas, and informative exhibits showcasing its rich history.

Take a guided tour, enjoy a meal at one of the onboard restaurants, or simply soak in the nostalgic ambiance as you wander the decks.

Museum Boijmans Van Beuningen:

Art enthusiasts will be captivated by the Museum Boijmans Van Beuningen, home to an extensive collection of artworks spanning centuries. From Old Masters to contemporary pieces, the museum showcases an eclectic range of art forms and styles.

Explore masterpieces by renowned artists such as Hieronymus Bosch, Salvador Dalí, and Vincent van Gogh, and immerse yourself in the world of art and culture.

Rotterdam's iconic landmarks and attractions embody the city's spirit of innovation, artistry, and architectural ingenuity. From the futuristic allure of the Erasmusbrug and Markthal to the historical significance of the Cube Houses and SS Rotterdam, each landmark tells a story, inviting visitors to delve deeper into Rotterdam's multifaceted character. Embark on a journey of exploration, and let the captivating allure of these iconic landmarks leave an indelible impression on your Rotterdam adventure.

CHAPTER SEVEN

Museums and Cultural Institutions

Rotterdam's rich cultural scene is a vibrant tapestry of museums and cultural institutions that invite visitors to immerse themselves in art, history, design, and innovation. From world-class art museums to cutting-edge exhibitions, Rotterdam's cultural offerings cater to a diverse range of interests and ignite the imagination. Join us as we explore some of the prominent museums and cultural institutions that make Rotterdam a haven for art enthusiasts, history buffs, and curious minds alike.

Museum Boijmans Van Beuningen:

As one of the Netherlands' oldest museums, the Museum Boijmans Van Beuningen boasts an exceptional collection spanning over 8,000 artworks from various periods.

Delve into the world of Dutch and European masterpieces, from the works of Rembrandt and Van Gogh to contemporary artists like Salvador Dalí and Piet Mondrian.

The museum's diverse exhibits encompass paintings, sculptures, prints, applied art, and design, offering a comprehensive art experience for all.

Kunsthal Rotterdam:

A hub of contemporary art and culture, the Kunsthal Rotterdam stands as a dynamic platform for diverse exhibitions, showcasing works across a wide range of disciplines.

Explore thought-provoking exhibitions featuring modern art, photography, design, fashion, and more, curated to challenge and inspire visitors.

With its ever-changing program, the Kunsthal ensures a fresh and engaging experience with each visit.

Maritime Museum Rotterdam:

Celebrating Rotterdam's maritime heritage, the Maritime Museum Rotterdam offers a fascinating journey through the city's seafaring past.

Explore interactive exhibitions, historical artifacts, and immersive displays that delve into topics such as shipbuilding, ports, trade, and the impact of maritime exploration on society.

Step aboard the historic ships moored at the museum's harbor, such as the SS Rotterdam and the submarine O-13, and gain a firsthand experience of maritime life.

Nederlands Fotomuseum:

For photography enthusiasts, the Nederlands Fotomuseum is a treasure trove, dedicated to preserving and showcasing Dutch photography from past to present.

Immerse yourself in captivating exhibitions that capture pivotal moments in history, evoke emotions, and provoke reflection through the lens of talented photographers.

From documentary photography to conceptual works, the museum celebrates the power of visual storytelling.

Het Nieuwe Instituut:

At the forefront of design, architecture, and digital culture, Het Nieuwe Instituut serves as a platform for innovation and exploration.

Engage with thought-provoking exhibitions, lectures, and events that explore the intersection of design, technology, and society.

Gain insights into the evolution of architecture, urban planning, and the impact of design on our daily lives.

Museum Rotterdam:

Museum Rotterdam is dedicated to preserving and showcasing the city's history and culture, offering a glimpse into Rotterdam's transformation over the centuries.

Explore interactive displays, historical objects, and multimedia exhibits that highlight Rotterdam's resilience, multiculturalism, and its role as a major port city.

Engage with stories of the city's inhabitants, past and present, and gain a deeper understanding of Rotterdam's identity.

Rotterdam's museums and cultural institutions form a vibrant tapestry, inviting visitors to explore the realms of art, history, design, and innovation. Whether you seek classical masterpieces, contemporary art, maritime heritage, or thought-provoking exhibitions, Rotterdam offers a diverse range of cultural experiences. Immerse yourself in this cultural oasis, and let the museums and institutions of Rotterdam ignite your curiosity and leave you with a deeper appreciation for the city's rich heritage and artistic spirit.

CHAPTER EIGHT

Food and Drink

Prepare your taste buds for a delectable journey through Rotterdam's vibrant food scene, where Dutch cuisine, local specialties, and a thriving culinary landscape await. From traditional flavors to international influences, Rotterdam offers a diverse array of dining experiences to satisfy every palate. Join us as we delve into the delights of Dutch cuisine, uncover must-visit restaurants and cafes, and explore the bustling food markets and street food scene that make Rotterdam a haven for food enthusiasts.

Dutch Cuisine and Local Specialties:

Dutch cuisine embodies a hearty and comforting culinary tradition, influenced by the country's rich agricultural heritage and seafaring traditions. Indulge in some beloved local specialties that reflect the essence of Dutch gastronomy.

Sample "stroopwafels," a beloved treat consisting of two thin waffles with a caramel-like syrup filling, best enjoyed warm. These sweet delights are a true Dutch indulgence.

Try "haring," the iconic Dutch herring, traditionally served raw with onions and pickles. Immerse yourself in the Dutch culture by embracing this unique and flavorsome street food experience.

Don't miss out on "bitterballen," delectable deep-fried meatballs with a crispy outer layer and a tender, flavorful interior. These bite-sized snacks are perfect for sharing and pair wonderfully with a cold Dutch beer.

Must-Visit Restaurants and Cafes:
Rotterdam boasts an exciting culinary scene, with a wide range of restaurants and cafes that cater to all tastes and preferences. Whether you're seeking fine dining experiences or casual eateries, Rotterdam has something to offer.

De Hef, a renowned restaurant located in the iconic Hef bridge, offers a unique dining experience with its panoramic views of the city and a menu featuring innovative Dutch cuisine with a modern twist.

Restaurant FG, headed by Michelin-starred chef François Geurds, showcases a culinary journey that combines molecular gastronomy, seasonal ingredients, and exquisite flavors, resulting in a truly unforgettable dining experience.

For a more laid-back atmosphere, explore the trendy Witte de Withstraat, a street lined with charming cafes and eateries. Enjoy artisanal coffee, indulge in homemade pastries, or savor international flavors from the eclectic mix of restaurants in the area.

Food Markets and Street Food:

Immerse yourself in the vibrant culinary scene of Rotterdam by visiting its bustling food markets and sampling delicious street food offerings.

The Markthal, an architectural marvel mentioned earlier, is not only a feast for the eyes but also a haven for food lovers. Explore the diverse range of fresh produce, local delicacies, and international flavors available under one roof.

On Tuesdays and Saturdays, visit the Rotterdam Market at Binnenrotte for a lively experience. Browse through stalls brimming with seasonal fruits, vegetables, cheeses, and more. Don't forget to try "kibbeling," a popular Dutch street food consisting of bite-sized pieces of fried fish served with tangy sauce.

Wander through the Fenix Food Factory, a warehouse-turned-food hall, where you can enjoy artisanal products, craft beers, and delectable snacks from local vendors. Experience the vibrant atmosphere and the passion that goes into Rotterdam's emerging food scene.

Rotterdam's food and drink offerings provide a tantalizing blend of Dutch flavors, international cuisines, and a thriving culinary culture. From indulging in local specialties like stroopwafels and haring to savoring the creations of acclaimed chefs at fine dining establishments, to immersing yourself in the lively atmosphere of food markets and street food, Rotterdam offers a gastronomic adventure that is sure to leave you craving for more. So, embark on this culinary journey and discover the delightful tastes and vibrant food culture that make Rotterdam a true food lover's paradise.

CHAPTER NINE

Shopping and Entertainment

In Rotterdam, retail therapy takes on a whole new meaning as the city offers a diverse shopping landscape, from popular shopping streets to unique boutiques and concept stores. But the excitement doesn't end there. As night falls, Rotterdam transforms into a vibrant hub of nightlife and entertainment. Join us as we dive into the world of shopping, uncover hidden gems, and explore the lively entertainment options that make Rotterdam a true urban playground.

Popular Shopping Streets and Areas:

Rotterdam is a shopper's paradise, with an array of popular streets and areas that cater to all tastes and styles.

Lijnbaan, one of Europe's first pedestrianized shopping streets, is a bustling hub featuring a mix of high-street brands, fashion boutiques, and department stores. Stroll along this vibrant street and discover the latest fashion trends.

Witte de Withstraat, mentioned earlier as a food destination, also offers a unique shopping experience. This artistic street is lined with independent boutiques, design stores, and art galleries, allowing you to indulge in a blend of fashion and culture.

Unique Boutiques and Concept Stores:

Rotterdam is a city known for its creative spirit, and this is reflected in its collection of unique boutiques and concept stores.

The Van Oldenbarneveltstraat, often referred to as Rotterdam's "Fashion Street," is home to a curated selection of high-end boutiques and designer stores. Explore this stylish street and discover exclusive fashion pieces that reflect Rotterdam's cutting-edge style.

For those seeking one-of-a-kind finds, head to the Nieuwe Binnenweg, a street filled with vintage shops, retro boutiques, and quirky concept stores. Unearth hidden treasures, from vintage clothing to antique furniture, and embrace Rotterdam's eclectic charm.

Nightlife and Entertainment Options:

When the sun sets, Rotterdam comes alive with an electric nightlife scene, offering a range of entertainment options for all preferences.

The Witte de Withstraat transforms into a buzzing hub of bars, clubs, and live music venues. Immerse yourself in the energetic atmosphere, enjoy a craft cocktail, and dance the night away to live performances or DJ sets.

Venture to the Kop van Zuid district and visit the trendy venues housed in the iconic De Rotterdam building. From rooftop bars offering panoramic views of the city to upscale lounges with innovative cocktails, you'll find the perfect spot to unwind and enjoy the city's skyline.

For a dose of culture, Rotterdam's theater scene provides a variety of performances, from theater plays and dance shows to concerts and opera. The Luxor Theater and the Rotterdamse Schouwburg are renowned venues that host a diverse range of productions throughout the year.

Rotterdam offers a dynamic fusion of shopping and entertainment, providing endless opportunities for exploration and enjoyment. From popular shopping streets like Lijnbaan to the unique boutiques and concept stores of Van Oldenbarneveltstraat and Nieuwe Binnenweg, Rotterdam caters to every shopper's desires. And when the sun sets, the city's vibrant nightlife scene comes alive, offering an array of bars, clubs, and cultural performances. So, indulge in some retail therapy, embrace the city's creative spirit, and immerse yourself in the lively entertainment options that make Rotterdam a true urban playground.

CHAPTER TEN

Events and Festivals that Ignite the City

In Rotterdam, the city's pulse quickens with an electrifying lineup of events and festivals that celebrate its diverse culture, artistic prowess, and innovative spirit. From lively music festivals that make your heart race to captivating art exhibitions that stir your imagination, Rotterdam is a city that knows how to throw a party. Join us as we unearth some of the most intriguing events and festivals that will arouse your senses and leave you with lasting memories.

Rotterdam Unlimited:

Rotterdam Unlimited is a dazzling celebration of music, dance, and cultural diversity. This vibrant festival takes over the city, inviting locals and visitors alike to revel in the rhythms of the world. Get ready for colorful parades, energetic street performances, and electrifying music stages where genres like jazz, reggae, salsa, and hip-hop take center stage. Feel the rhythm pulsating through your veins and join the crowd as they dance and celebrate the unity of cultures.

International Film Festival Rotterdam (IFFR):

Film enthusiasts flock to Rotterdam for the International Film Festival Rotterdam (IFFR), one of the most important film events in the world. With a focus on innovative and daring cinema, IFFR showcases a diverse range of films, from thought-provoking documentaries to avant-garde masterpieces. Immerse yourself in the cinematic world, attending screenings, engaging in Q&A sessions with filmmakers, and exploring the festival's vibrant atmosphere that buzzes with creative energy.

North Sea Jazz Festival:

For music aficionados, the North Sea Jazz Festival is an unparalleled experience. Renowned as one of the world's premier jazz events, this three-day festival draws top-tier artists from across the globe. From legendary jazz icons to emerging talents, the festival's stages come alive with mesmerizing performances spanning jazz, soul, funk, and more. Lose yourself in the soulful melodies, savor the atmosphere of musical camaraderie, and witness the magic of world-class musicians taking jazz to new heights.

Rotterdam Art Week:

Art enthusiasts rejoice during Rotterdam Art Week, a celebration of contemporary art that transforms the city into a cultural playground. This week-long event showcases a wide array of artistic disciplines, including visual arts, installations, performances, and immersive experiences. Wander through art exhibitions, discover cutting-edge installations, and engage in thought-provoking conversations with artists, curators, and fellow art lovers. Rotterdam Art Week will ignite your imagination and leave you inspired by the boundless creativity within the city.

World Port Days:

As the "Gateway to Europe," Rotterdam celebrates its maritime heritage and global connections during the World Port Days. This festival allows visitors to get an up-close look at the city's bustling port and its impressive ships. Enjoy thrilling boat tours, witness awe-inspiring demonstrations, and experience the energy of the maritime industry firsthand. Immerse yourself in the vibrant atmosphere, and marvel at the immense scale of Rotterdam's port operations.

In Rotterdam, the city's events and festivals create a vibrant tapestry of cultural celebration, artistic exploration, and joyful moments. Whether you're dancing to the beats of Rotterdam Unlimited, immersing yourself in the cinematic world of IFFR, or losing yourself in the soulful melodies of the North Sea Jazz Festival, these events and festivals will ignite your spirit and leave you craving more. So mark your calendar, immerse yourself in the festive rhythms of Rotterdam, and let the city's dynamic events and festivals elevate your experience to new heights.

CHAPTER ELEVEN

Outdoor Activities and Parks

While Rotterdam is renowned for its impressive architecture and urban energy, the city also offers an abundance of outdoor activities and serene parks that allow you to reconnect with nature and embrace the great outdoors. From tranquil gardens to expansive forests, Rotterdam invites you to embark on outdoor adventures that will rejuvenate your soul. Join us as we explore the breathtaking beauty of Het Park, the tranquil oasis of Kralingse Bos, the captivating world of Rotterdam Zoo and Blijdorp Gardens, and the cycling and walking routes that showcase the city's natural wonders.

Het Park:

Step into Het Park, a serene and picturesque green space nestled on the banks of the Maas River. This park, dating back to the 19th century, offers a tranquil escape from the bustling city.

Enjoy leisurely walks along tree-lined paths, breathe in the fresh air, and take in the panoramic views of the river and the iconic Euromast. Discover hidden corners where you can relax and unwind amidst the beauty of nature.

Kralingse Bos:

Immerse yourself in nature's embrace at Kralingse Bos, a sprawling forest and lake area that serves as the city's backyard. Spanning over 200 hectares, this verdant oasis offers a variety of outdoor activities for all.

Take a leisurely stroll or jog along the scenic trails that wind through the forest, or rent a paddleboat to explore the tranquil lake. Pack a picnic and find a cozy spot under the shade of trees, or simply bask in the serenity of nature.

Rotterdam Zoo and Blijdorp Gardens:

Rotterdam Zoo, or Diergaarde Blijdorp is not only a haven for animal lovers but also a beautiful space that blends nature and wildlife conservation.

Explore the stunning Blijdorp Gardens within the zoo, featuring beautifully manicured landscapes, colorful flower beds, and serene ponds. Take a leisurely stroll and embrace the tranquility that surrounds you.

Visit the Butterfly Paradise, mentioned earlier, and witness the vibrant fluttering wings of butterflies in this tropical greenhouse. It's a magical experience that connects you with the delicate beauty of these creatures.

Cycling and Walking Routes:

Rotterdam is a cyclist's paradise, with a network of well-maintained cycling and walking routes that allow you to explore the city's natural and urban landscapes.

Embark on the Rotterdam River Route and cycle along the banks of the Maas River, enjoying stunning waterfront views and passing by iconic landmarks.

For a more rural experience, venture into the outskirts of Rotterdam and discover the Rottemeren area. This picturesque landscape offers scenic cycling and walking trails, passing by lakes, windmills, and charming Dutch villages.

Rotterdam's outdoor activities and parks provide a sanctuary of serenity within the urban landscape. Whether you choose to wander through the enchanting pathways of Het Park, immerse yourself in the tranquility of Kralingse Bos, explore the captivating world of Rotterdam Zoo and Blijdorp Gardens, or embark on cycling and walking routes that showcase the city's natural beauty, you'll find yourself immersed in the wonders of nature. So, embrace the opportunity to rejuvenate your spirit, reconnect with the outdoors, and create lasting memories amidst Rotterdam's breathtaking outdoor playgrounds.

CHAPTER TWELVE

Day Trips from Rotterdam

While Rotterdam captivates visitors with its modern architecture and vibrant city life, the surrounding region offers a treasure trove of day trip opportunities that allow you to delve into Dutch history, culture, and picturesque landscapes. Join us as we embark on unforgettable journeys to the charming city of Delft, the regal city of The Hague, the enchanting windmills of Kinderdijk, and the historic town of Gouda. Get ready to immerse yourself in the rich heritage and scenic wonders that await just a short distance from Rotterdam.

Delft:

Step into the enchanting world of Delft, a city famed for its picturesque canals, historic architecture, and its renowned Delftware pottery.

Stroll through the charming streets of the old town, lined with beautiful gabled houses and quaint boutiques. Visit the iconic Oude Kerk (Old Church) and the Nieuwe Kerk (New Church) with stunning views from the tower.

Immerse yourself in Delftware's rich history and craftsmanship at the Royal Delft factory. Witness the intricate process of creating these blue and white ceramics and explore the museum to learn more about their significance in Dutch culture.

The Hague:

Discover the regal allure of The Hague, the political capital of the Netherlands and a city renowned for its international importance and cultural landmarks.

Explore the impressive Binnenhof, the historic heart of Dutch politics, and marvel at the architectural grandeur of the Peace Palace, home to the International Court of Justice.

Lose yourself in the art and history at the Mauritshuis, a renowned museum housing masterpieces by Vermeer, Rembrandt, and other Dutch masters. Take a stroll along the scenic Scheveningen beach and indulge in seaside delights.

Kinderdijk:

Venture into the Dutch countryside and witness the iconic windmills of Kinderdijk, a UNESCO World Heritage site and a testament to the country's age-old battle against the water.

Marvel at the 19 beautifully preserved windmills, standing in perfect harmony amidst the polders and canals. Take a boat tour or rent a bicycle to explore the area, learning about the history and engineering behind these majestic structures.

Gouda:

Delight in the historic charm of Gouda, a picturesque town known for its cheese, charming canals, and stunning Gothic architecture.

Visit the majestic Gouda City Hall, stroll through the Markt Square, and marvel at the Gothic-style St.

Janskerk, famous for its mesmerizing stained glass windows.

Don't miss the opportunity to taste the world-famous Gouda cheese at the Cheese Market, held during the summer months, and explore the quaint streets lined with cheese shops and boutiques.

Just a stone's throw away from Rotterdam, Delft, The Hague, Kinderdijk, and Gouda beckon with their unique charms and fascinating history. These day-trip destinations offer a glimpse into the rich cultural heritage and scenic wonders of the Netherlands. So, take a break from the bustling city and embark on these unforgettable journeys, where you'll uncover hidden treasures, experience Dutch traditions, and create lasting memories in the enchanting surroundings of Delft, The Hague, Kinderdijk, and Gouda.

CHAPTER THIRTEEN

Practical Information for a Seamless Rotterdam Experience

To ensure a seamless and enjoyable visit to Rotterdam, it's essential to familiarize yourself with practical information that will enhance your trip. From understanding the weather patterns and the best time to visit to managing currency and banking needs, as well as prioritizing safety and emergency preparedness, this guide will equip you with the knowledge you need. Additionally, we'll provide you with some useful phrases in Dutch to enhance your interactions with locals and create memorable experiences.

Weather and Best Time to Visit:

Rotterdam experiences a moderate maritime climate, with mild summers and cool winters. Be prepared for occasional rainfall throughout the year.

The best time to visit Rotterdam is during the spring (April to June) and autumn (September to October) seasons when the weather is generally pleasant, and the city comes alive with vibrant festivals and events.

Currency and Banking:

The official currency in the Netherlands is the Euro (€). Currency exchange services are readily available at airports, banks, and exchange offices throughout the city.

Major credit and debit cards are widely accepted in Rotterdam. ATMs are easily accessible for cash withdrawals, but it's advisable to inform your bank of your travel plans to avoid any card issues.

Safety Tips and Emergency Numbers:

Rotterdam is generally a safe city, but it's always wise to take precautions. Be mindful of your belongings and avoid displaying valuable items in crowded areas.

In case of an emergency, dial the following numbers:

- Police: 112
- Ambulance and Fire Department: 112

Useful Phrases in Dutch:

Interacting with locals in their native language can greatly enhance your experience. Here are some useful Dutch phrases to get you started:

- Hello: Hallo
- Thank you: Dank je wel
- Excuse me: Pardon
- Please: Alsjeblieft
- Do you speak English?: Spreekt u Engels?
- Where is...?: Waar is...?
- Goodbye: Tot ziens

Equipped with practical information, you're now ready to embark on a seamless Rotterdam adventure. Consider the weather patterns and choose the best time to visit, manage your currency and banking needs efficiently, prioritize safety by staying vigilant, and be prepared with emergency numbers. Additionally, mastering a few useful phrases in Dutch will enhance your interactions with locals and demonstrate your appreciation for their culture. So, armed with knowledge and preparedness, dive into the vibrant atmosphere of Rotterdam and create unforgettable memories.

Conclusion

Recap of Rotterdam's Highlights

Throughout this guide, we have explored the captivating city of Rotterdam, delving into its rich tapestry of attractions, culture, and natural wonders. Let's take a moment to recap the highlights that make Rotterdam an extraordinary destination:

- Marvel at the architectural marvels like the Erasmus Bridge, Markthal, and Cube Houses that redefine the cityscape.

- Immerse yourself in the vibrant cultural scene, from world-class museums like the Kunsthal to the buzzing Witte de Withstraat.

- Explore the city's diverse neighborhoods, each offering a unique ambiance and charm, from the cosmopolitan vibe of the city center to the historic streets of Delfshaven.

- Reconnect with nature in the tranquil parks, embrace the beauty of the windmills at Kinderdijk, and embark on cycling and walking routes that unveil the city's natural splendor.

- Indulge in delectable Dutch cuisine, visit local markets, and experience the warmth and hospitality of Rotterdam's food scene.

Final Tips and Suggestions for Visitors

- Embrace the spirit of adventure and wander off the beaten path. Rotterdam has hidden gems tucked away in unexpected corners.

- Engage with the locals and embrace their warm hospitality. Rotterdam is a city that thrives on its diverse community and their stories.

- Pack comfortable shoes and be prepared to explore the city on foot or by bike, immersing yourself in the vibrant atmosphere at every turn.

- Check the local event calendars for festivals, exhibitions, and cultural events happening during your visit. Rotterdam's calendar is always brimming with exciting happenings.

- Don't be afraid to ask for recommendations. Locals are proud of their city and are often more than happy to share their favorite spots and insider tips.

- Lastly, embrace the unique spirit of Rotterdam—its resilience, creativity, and willingness to embrace change. Let the city's dynamic energy inspire you and leave you with memories that will last a lifetime.

Rotterdam, a city that defies expectations, has revealed its enchanting allure through its iconic landmarks, cultural institutions, parks, and vibrant culinary scene. From the awe-inspiring architecture to the warm hospitality of its residents, Rotterdam offers a tapestry of experiences that will leave you captivated. As you bid farewell to this remarkable city, take with you the memories of its vibrant streets, the stories of its people, and the spirit of

Rotterdam's continuous reinvention. Embrace the opportunity to explore, discover, and connect with this remarkable destination, for Rotterdam is a city that will forever hold a special place in your heart.

Printed in Great Britain
by Amazon

52077523R00046